FULFILLING PURPOSE

52 Divine Affirmations: Shaping
Destiny

BY

SYLVIA C. OBIEFULE

FULFILLING PURPOSE

ACKNOWLEDGEMENT

I would like to acknowledge the El-Shaddai, Elohim. The God who sees me. The Architect of my life's journey; my Shield, my glory and the Lifter up of my head. Alleluia!

Pastor and Mrs. Edward Kwakye of Faithway Baptist Church Brice Ohio, for your invaluable support.

To Dr. Mike Okonkwo, The Presiding Bishop TREM International Nigeria for giving me the foundation to knowing the Word.

To Dr. Daniel O. Ajayi; thank you for all your support.

To Jude O. Obiefule. Thank you for making out time to proof-reading. May God lift you beyond your expectations in Jesus name Amen.

PREFACE

When satan tempted Jesus to eat bread while fasting in Mathew 4:4 *Jesus answered, Man shall not live by bread alone but by every word that proceeds out of the mouth of God.* The world we live in today demands a daily confession of God's Word to give life, shape purpose and destiny. If you can "eat" the Word daily, surely, you will never go hungry or thirst. The Word is Jesus made flesh. He is the fountain of Life, the Way, the Truth and Life. There is no life without the Word which is God himself.

The Word never fails. The way to your greatness, your success is the Word! To fulfill purpose, you need the Word! Declare the Word daily and watch God confirm and perform His Word. For with God, all things are possible. You shall fulfill purpose in Jesus name. Amen.

CONTENTS

Week Fifty-One

Unbeatable Peace

Week Fifty-Two

I Live.

Theme: Believe!

Text: Psalm 3:3, Psalm 43:19,

Psalm 34:4,10, Ephesians 6:10,

Philippians 4:13,2Timothy 1:17,

Psalm 1:3, Genesis 13:15.

Affirmation

The Lord is my strong tower, in Him I am safe and set on high. He is my shield, my glory and the lifter up of my head. He shall order my steps and I shall never fall into the traps of the enemy.

Behold the Lord will do a new thing in my life, now it shall spring forth. He shall make ways in my wilderness and rivers of water in my deserts. I shall be like a tree planted by streams of water. I shall yield fruits in season, and my leaf will never wither. I will prosper in all I do.

I delight myself in the Lord and He shall fulfill the desires of my heart. As I seek the Lord today, I shall not lack any good thing. I am strong in the Lord and in the power of His might. I can do all things through Christ that strengthens me. For God has not given me the spirit of fear but of power, of love and of sound mind. As far as my eyes can see, the Lord has given unto me and my seed forever. I shall fulfill purpose in Jesus name Amen!

Theme: **His Thoughts for Me!**

Text: Jeremiah 29:11, Isiah 55:8,

1 Peter 5:7, Psalm 29:11,

Isaiah 55:12, Isiah 51:3,

Isiah 54:10,

Affirmation

For the Lord knows the thoughts He thinks towards me. He has a plan for me, thoughts of peace and not evil, to give me a future and hope. For His thoughts are not my thoughts or my ways His ways. I cast all my anxiety on Him because He cares for me.

The Lord gives me strength and blesses me with peace. Therefore, I shall go out in joy and be led out in peace. The mountains and the hills shall break forth into singing before me, and all the trees of the field shall clap their hands. The Lord shall comfort all my waste places. He will make my wilderness to blossom and my desert like the garden of the Lord. Joy and gladness, thanksgiving and the voice of melody shall be found in me.

Though the mountains shall depart, and the hills be removed, but Your kindness shall not depart from me, neither shall your covenant of peace be removed. The peace of God which transcends all understanding will guard my heart and my mind shall always stay on You. I shall fulfill purpose in Jesus name Amen

Theme: Secured and Blessed

Text: Proverbs 18:10, Psalm 91:9-10,

Psalm 118:17, Philippians 1:6,

Proverbs 23:18, proverbs 3:9-10,

Affirmation

The name of the Lord is a strong tower; I run into it and I am safe. As the mountains surround Jerusalem, the Lord will be a shield to me and my family. Because I have made the Lord my refuge even the Most High my dwelling place, therefore no evil shall befall me nor shall any plague near my dwelling. No counsel of the wicked against me or my family shall stand. I shall not die but will live to declare the works of the Lord. I am confident that He that begun the good work in me shall complete it . For surely there is an end and my expectations shall not be cut off. As I honor the Lord with my possessions, and the first fruit of all my increase, so my barn will be filled with plenty and my vats will overflow with new wine. I shall fulfill purpose in Jesus name Amen

Week Four

Theme: The Rain

Text: Joel 2:23-24, Psalm 23

Affirmation

I rejoice in the Lord my God for He has given me the former rain faithfully; and He will cause the rain to come down for me: the former rain and the latter rain in this first month. My threshing floors shall be full of wheat and my vats shall overflow with new wine and oil. The Lord is my Shepherd. I shall not want. He makes me lie down in green pastures; He leads me beside the still waters He restores my soul. He leads me in the paths of righteousness, for His name's sake. Yea tough I walk through the valley of shadow of death, I will fear no evil, for you are with me, your rod and your staff, they comfort me. You prepare a table before me in the presence of my enemies, you anoint my head with oil, my cup runs over. Surely goodness and mercy shall follow me, all the days of my life. And I will dwell in the house of the Lord forever, I shall fulfill purpose in Jesus name Amen!

Theme: It Shall Come to Pass

Text: Habakkuk 2:3, Romans 8:28,

Psalm 30:6-7, Psalm 33:11,

Proverbs 19:21, Acts 17:28.

Affirmation:

For the vision the Lord has given to me is yet for an appointed time, but at the end it shall speak, and not lie: though it tarries, I will wait for it because it will surely come, it will not fail.

All things work together for my good, because I love God and am called according to His purpose. Even in my prosperity, I shall not be moved. Lord by your favor you have made my mountain to stand strong. There are many devises in the man's heart, nevertheless the counsel of the Lord over my life and family shall stand. The counsel of the Lord stands forever. In

Him I live and move and have my being. In Him I will fulfill this vision, in Him I shall fulfill purpose in Jesus name Amen.

Theme: Overcomer in Christ

Text: Jeremiah 1:10, Galatians 5: 16-18,
2 Corinthians 10:5, Romans 8:1,
1 John 4:4

Affirmation

The Lord has this day set before me over nations and over kingdoms. I root out every corrupt seed in my life that will be a barrier to possessing my possessions this year. I pull down every stronghold of the devil and everything that exalts itself above God in my life. I overcome every lust of the flesh (fornication, drunkenness, lies, anger, envy, jealousy, hatred, adultery etc) in the name of Jesus.

I am a new creation in Christ Jesus, I walk not in the flesh, I am not under the law but am led by the Spirit. For there is no condemnation for those who are in Christ Jesus who walk not

in the flesh but in the spirit. I shall
fulfill purpose in Jesus name.!!!! Amen.

Week Seven

Theme: Lifted

Text: Psalm 27:1-5

Affirmation

The Lord is my light and my salvation whom shall, I fear? The Lord is the strength of my life of whom shall I be afraid of. When the wicked came against me to eat up my flesh, my enemies and foes, they stumbled and fell.

Though an army may encamp against me, my heart shall not fear. Though war may rise against me, in this I will be confident: one thing I have desired of the Lord, that I will seek that I may dwell in the house of the Lord, all the days of my life. To behold the beauty of the Lord and to inquire in His temple. For in time of trouble He shall hide me in His pavilion. In the secret place of His tabernacle He shall hide me, He shall set me high upon a rock. I am lifted by the Lord from every destruction and pain. I shall fulfill destiny in Jesus name Amen.

Week Eight

Theme: Royalty

Text: Galatians. 2:20, 2 Peter 1:3,

Revelation 1:6, 1 Peter 2:9)

Affirmation

I am crucified with Christ: nevertheless, I live; yet not I, but Christ lives in me: and the life which I live in the flesh I live by faith of the son of God who loved me and gave Himself for me.

According as His divine power, He has given unto me all things that pertain unto life and godliness, through the knowledge of him that has called me to glory and virtue. And has made me a King and a priest unto God and His Father, I am a royal Priesthood, a holy nation, a peculiar person, I shall show forth the praises of Him who hath called me out of darkness into His marvelous light, to him be glory and dominion forever and ever Amen.

Theme: Secured in His Mercy

Text: Psalms 103:1-5,34:1-2; 118:14 &

17; 138:8, Isaiah 40:31

Affirmation

Bless the Lord Oh my soul, and all that is within me bless His holy name! Bless the Lord o my soul and forget not of all His benefits: who forgives all my iniquities, who heals all my diseases, who redeems my life from destruction, who crowns me with loving kindness and tender mercies, who satisfies my mouth with good things so that my youth is renewed like the eagle.

I will always bless the Lord; His praises shall continually be in my mouth. My soul shall make its boast in the Lord for He has become my salvation. I shall not die but I shall live to declare the works of my Lord. For He shall perfect all that concerns me. I will wait upon the Lord so shall my strength be renewed daily. I shall fulfill purpose in Jesus name Amen.

Theme: Blessed and Highly Favored

Text: Psalm 37:4, Psalm 1:3,

Isaiah 8:18. Psalm 1:2-3; 5:12; 6:6,

2 Corinthians 3:18.

Affirmation

My delight is in the Lord and He fulfills the desires of my heart. I am fruitful and shall bring forth fruits in my seasons. My leaves shall ever remain green.

Because my delight is in the word of God and I meditate it day and night, I am like a tree planted by the rivers of waters that brings forth its fruit in due season, whose leaves also shall not wither and whatever I do shall prosper.

I and my children are for signs and wonders. Therefore, whatever I do, wherever I go, signs and wonders shall follow me. I am blessed going out, I am blessed coming in. The Lord shall surround me with favor like a shield. Lines have fallen to me in pleasant places YEA! I have a good inheritance. I am blessed and highly favored in Jesus name Amen.

Theme: Indestructible in Jesus Christ

Text: Psalm 27:1, Isaiah 43:1-2,

Acts 17:28 Isaiah 54:10;17

Affirmation

The Lord is my light and my salvation whom shall, I fear? He is the strength of my life of whom shall I be afraid of? He has redeemed me and has called me by my name. I am His. Even when I go through the waters, He is with me and through the rivers, they shall not overflow me. When I walk through the fire, it will not burn me, nor shall the flame scorch me. For the Lord is my savior, He is with me. In Him I live and move and have my being.

I let the peace of Christ rule over my heart. His grace is enough for me, for His strength is made perfect in my weakness. I am more than a conqueror; I am victorious in Christ Jesus. No weapon formed against me shall prosper. I condemn every tongue speaking against me in judgement. I am blessed and cannot be cursed. I shall fulfill purpose in Jesus name Amen.

Theme: Fully Restored

Text: Psalms 23:1-3, Isaiah 62:3-4,

Isaiah 60:18, John 7:38,

Psalm 23: 6)

Affirmation

The Lord is my shepherd I shall not want, He makes me to lie down in green pastures. He leads me beside the still waters. He restores my soul: He leads me in the paths of righteousness for His name's sake.

I am a crown of glory in the hand of the Lord and a royal diadem in Him. I shall no more be termed forsaken nor shall my land be desolate, but I shall be called Hephzibah and my land Beulah. Violence shall no longer be heard in my land, neither wasting nor destruction in my territory. My walls are called Salvation and my gates

Praise. Out of my belly shall flow rivers of living waters. Surely goodness and mercy shall follow me all the days of my life and. I shall dwell in the house of my God forever and ever in Jesus name Amen.

Theme: Understanding Sets Apart

Text: Ephesians 1:3, 1Chronicle 12:32,

Ephesians 1:17-18,

2 Corinthians 12:9,1 Kings 3:12)

Affirmation

Blessed be the God and Father of our Lord Jesus Christ who has blessed me with every spiritual blessing in the heavenly places in Christ. I am blessed and highly favored.

I receive the spirit of understanding like the sons of Issachar to know exactly what I need to do at the right time. I receive the spirit of wisdom and revelation in the knowledge of Him, to open my eyes of understanding that I may know what the hope of His calling and the riches of the glory of His inheritance in the saints is. I receive grace to do the extraordinary. The Lord shall give me a wise and

discerning mind so that none like me
has been before and none like me shall
arise after me. I am one of a kind. I shall
fulfill purpose in Jesus name Amen.

Theme: Multiple Blessings.

Text: Isaiah 61:7, Joel 2:25-26,

Zacharia 8:12, Psalm 71:21

Affirmation

Instead of shame I shall have double honor and instead of confusion, I shall rejoice in my portion. Therefore, in this land, I shall possess double, everlasting joy shall be mine.

The Lord is restoring all the years the locust, palmerworm and cankerworm have stolen in my life. I am fruitful and shall bear good fruits in this land. I shall not lack but shall eat in plenty and be satisfied. My seeds shall be prosperous, my vine shall give its fruits, the ground shall give her increase and the heavens shall give their dew. The Lord will cause me to possess all these things. He shall increase my greatness and comfort me

on every side. I live from glory to glory;
I shall fulfill purpose in Jesus name
Amen.

Week Fifteen

Theme: Blessed Assurance

Text: Psalm 40:3, Genesis 15:1,

Psalm 35:27, Isaiah 43:1-3,

Psalm 23:4, Psalm 46:1,

1 Thessalonians 5:24.

Affirmation

I will bless the name of the Lord as long as I have breath in me. He has put a new song in my mouth, many shall see it and fear and trust in God. He is my shield and my shield and my exceedingly great reward.

Let the Lord be magnified who has pleasure in my prosperity; I am the seed of Abraham. He has called me by my name, I am His. When I go through the fire it will not burn me, when I go through the waters it will not swallow me up for, He has promised He is with me and can never forsake me. He is always there for me, with His crook and staff with that He gives me comfort. He is my present help in time of need. Faithful, is He that called me, who will also do it. I shall fulfill purpose in Jesus name Amen.

Theme: The King of Glory!

Text: Psalm 24:1-2,7-10, Psalm 91: 10,

Psalm 121: 6:8

Affirmation

The earth is the Lord's and the fullness there of. The world and those who dwell therein. For He founded it upon the seas and established it upon the waters. He is the anchor to my soul, the pillar of my life, the orchestrator of my life's journey.

Lift up your heads oh you gates and be lifted up you everlasting doors and the King of glory shall come in, who is this King of Glory? The Lord strong and Mighty, The Lord mighty in battle. Lift up your heads oh you gates! Lift up you everlasting door ! And the King of Glory shall come in. Who is this King of Glory ? The Lord of Hosts, He is the King of Glory. No evil shall come near me neither shall any plague come near my dwelling. For the Lord the Most High is my dwelling place. The sun shall not strike me by day nor the moon by night. I am blessed going out and I am blessed coming in. I shall fulfill purpose in Jesus name Amen.

Theme: Abiding in Him.

Text: Psalm 106:1, Psalm 121:3,

Isiah 60:20, John 15:4-7,

Psalm 1:3, Proverb 4:18

Affirmation

Thanks be to the Lord for He is good and His mercy endures forever. He will not suffer my foot to be moved. He that keeps me (mention your name) shall neither slumber nor sleep. My sun shall no longer go down nor shall my moon withdraw itself for the Lord will be my everlasting light and the days of my mourning shall be ended.

I am light, therefore no darkness will comprehend me. A city set on the mountain top that cannot be hidden. I abide in the Lord; the True Vine every day of my life. I abide in His word so I shall bear much fruit. I shall bring forth fruit and my desires shall be done for me. My leaves shall not wither and whatever I do shall prosper. My path is like a shining sun that shines ever brighter unto the perfect day. I shall fulfill purpose in Jesus name Amen.)

Week Eighteen

Theme: Fruitfulness in My Land.

Text: Leviticus 26:4-13.

Affirmation

The Lord shall give me rain in its season. The land shall yield its produce and the tress of the field shall yield their fruit. My threshing shall last till the time of vintage and the vintage shall last till the time of my sowing. I shall eat my bread to the full and dwell in my land safely.

The Lord will give peace to the land and I shall lie down and non will make me afraid. The Lord will rid the land of evil beasts and the sword will not go through my land. I will chase my enemies and they shall fall by the sword before me. He will look on me favorably and make me fruitful, multiply me and confirm my covenant with Him. He has delivered me from bondage. He has broken the bands of my yoke and made me walk uprightly. I am no longer a slave, but an heir to His Kingdom. I shall fulfill purpose in Jesus name Amen.

Theme: My Helper

Text: Psalm 121:1, Isaiah 41:10,

Isaiah 41:18, Isiah 40:29-30.

Affirmation

I will lift up my eyes to the hills, from whence comes my help? My help comes from the Lord who made heaven and earth. I shall not be afraid for the Lord is with me. I shall not be dismayed for He is my God. He will strengthen me, Yes, He will help me. He will uphold me with His righteous right hand.

The Lord will open rivers in my desolate heights, and fountains in the midst of valleys. He will make my wilderness a pool of water and the dry land springs of water. He gives me power and increases my strength. Even the youth shall faint and be weary and the young men shall utterly

fall, but I will wait on the Lord and I
shall renew my strength. I shall mount
up with wings like eagles. I shall run
and not be weary, I shall walk and not
faint. I shall fulfill purpose in Jesus
name Amen

Week Twenty

Theme: Blessed Beyond Curse

Text: Ephesians 1:3,1 Chronicle 12:32,

Ephesians 1:17-18,

2 Corinthians 12:9, 1 King 3:12

Proverbs 2:1-12

Affirmation

Blessed be the God and Father of our Lord Jesus Christ who has blessed me with every spiritual blessing in the heavenly places in Christ. I am blessed and highly favored.

I receive the spirit of understanding like the sons of Issachar to know exactly what I need to do at the right time. I receive the spirit of wisdom and revelation in the knowledge of Him, to open my eyes of understanding that I may know what the hope of His calling and the riches of the glory of

His inheritance in the saints is. I receive grace to do the extraordinary. The Lord shall give me a wise and discerning mind so that none like me has been before and none like me shall arise after me. Discretion will preserve me, and understanding will keep me and deliver me from the way of evil. I am one of a kind. I shall fulfill purpose in Jesus name Amen.

Theme: Delivered to Divine Inheritance

Text: Psalm 24:1, Daniel 2:20,

Haggai 2:8, Colossians 1:13,

Romans 8:7, 2 Peter1:3-4,

Isaiah 45:3, Psalm 84:11

Affirmation

The earth and all it contain; the world, wisdom and power, all belongs to God for ever and ever. Silver and gold are all His. I give all thanks to the Jesus who has qualified me to be a partaker of the inheritance of the saints in the light.

I walk in light; no darkness can comprehend me. He has delivered me from the power of darkness and conveyed me into His kingdom of light. I am an heir of His kingdom, a joint heir with Christ, a partaker of His divine nature. He empowers me to make wealth. He has given me all things that pertain to life and godliness. He shall open my eyes to the treasures in the darkness and secret riches in hidden places. I dwell in abundance. The Lord God is my sun and my shield. He will give me grace and glory. No good thing will He withhold from me. I shall fulfill purpose in Jesus name Amen.

Theme: Adopted Forever

Text: Psalm 27:1, Isaiah 43:1-2,

Acts 17:28 Isaiah 54:10:17,

Psalm 23:6

Affirmation

The Lord is my light and my salvation whom shall, I fear? He is the strength of my life of whom shall I be afraid of? He has redeemed me and has called me by my name. I am His.

Even when I go through the waters it will not swallow me up or through the fire, it will not burn me, For He is with me. In Him I live and move and have my being. His kindness shall not depart from me neither shall His covenant of peace be removed. I am blessed going out, I am blessed coming in. Surely goodness and mercy shall follow me all the days of my life and I

shall dwell in the house of the Lord for
ever and ever. No weapon formed
against me shall prosper. I condemn
every tongue speaking against me in
judgement. I am blessed and cannot be
cursed. I shall fulfill purpose in Jesus
name Amen.

Theme: Glorious Ending

Text: Psalm 138:1-2, Psalm 89:34,

Psalm 90-14; 16-17

Philippians 1:6, Psalm 138:8,

Proverbs 23:18, Psalm 37 :25

Affirmation

I will praise you with my whole heart, before the gods I will sing praises to you. I will worship towards your holy temple and praise your name, for Your loving kindness and Your truth. You have magnified your word above all your names. Great and mighty are you oh God! Your covenant you will never break nor alter the word that has gone out of your mouth.

Oh! satisfy me daily with your mercy that I may rejoice and be glad all my days. Oh Lord show me Your glory. Let Your beauty be upon me oh God and establish the work of my hands. One thing I am very confident, that You, who began a good work in me will complete it until the day of our Lord Jesus Christ.

Surely there is an end and my expectations shall not be cut off. I have never seen the righteous forsaken and his descendants begging for bread. You shall perfect all that concerns me. Your mercy endures forever. You shall not forsake the works of your hands. It is my season of manifestation. It is my season of new songs. I shall fulfill purpose in Jesus name Amen.

Theme: His Word Is Mighty in Me

Text: Isaiah 55:11, Isiah 40: 8:28,

Jeremiah 29:11, Isaiah 55:5,

Isaiah 60:10

Affirmation

God is mighty, the creator of the ends of the earth. His understanding is unsearchable, and His word is forever. Every word and promises God has made concerning me shall never return to Him void, but it shall accomplish what He pleases and shall prosper in the thing for which He sent it.

My God has plans for me. His thoughts towards me are thoughts of peace and not evil and to give me a future and an expected end. Even the youths shall faint and be weary and young men shall utterly fall. But as I wait on God, my strength is renewed. I shall mount up with wings like eagles, I shall run and not be weary, I shall walk and not faint. Nations who do not know me shall serve me for the Lord has glorified me. Strangers shall build my walls and their kings shall minister to me. I will fulfill purpose in Jesus name. Amen.

Theme: New Life in Christ

Text: Romans 8:1-2, Isaiah 42:9,

2 Corinthians 5:17,

Numbers 23:8:20, Isaiah 41:18

Affirmation

There is therefore now no condemnation for me in Christ Jesus; for I do not walk in flesh but in spirit. For the law of the spirit of life in Christ Jesus has made me free from the law of sin and death.

I do not remember the former things nor consider the things of the old. Behold the Lord is doing a new thing. It has started to spring forth. I am a new creature in Christ, old things have passed away. Behold all things have become new. I am blessed and cannot be cursed. He will open rivers in desolate heights for me and fountains in the midst of valleys. He will make my wilderness a pool of water and the dry land springs of water. It is my season of new opportunities. It is my season of greatness. I will fulfill purpose in Jesus name. Amen.

Theme: World Overcomer

Text: Psalm 18:32-37, Isaiah 54:17,

Ephesians 6:10, 1 John 4:4.

Affirmation

I will rejoice in the Lord. I will rejoice in the God of my salvation. You armed me with strength and make my ways perfect. You make my feet like the feet of deer and sets me on my high places. You teach my hands to make war so that my arms can bend a bow of bronze. You have also given me a shield of thy salvation and your right hand holds me up and your gentleness has made me great. You have enlarged my steps that my feet did not slip. I have pursued my enemies and overtaken them neither did I turn back again till they were destroyed. They have fallen under my feet.

No weapon of the enemy against me and my family shall prosper and every tongue that shall rise against me in judgement, I condemn. For this is my heritage in the Lord. I am strong in the Lord and in the power of His might. Greater is He that is in me. I shall fulfill destiny Amen.

Theme: Divine Inheritance

Text: Psalm 24:1, Daniel 2:20,

Haggai 2:8, Colossians 1:13,

Romans 8:7, 2 Peter1:3-4,

Isaiah 45:3.

Affirmation

The earth and all its contents, the world, wisdom and power, all belongs to God for ever and ever. Silver and gold are all His.

I give all thanks to the Jesus who has qualified me to be a partaker of the inheritance of the saints in the light. I walk in light; no darkness can comprehend me. He has delivered me from the power of darkness and conveyed me into His kingdom of light. I am an heir of His kingdom, a joint heir with Christ, a partaker of

His divine nature. He empowers me to make wealth. He has given me all things that pertain to life and godliness. He shall open my eyes to the treasures in the darkness and secret riches in hidden places. I am rich in Christ. I shall fulfill purpose in Jesus name Amen.

Theme: Fruitfulness in The Word

Text: Psalm 119:105, Psalm 3:3,

Proverbs 3:5-6, Psalm 1:2-3,

2 Corinthians 9:10

Affirmation

Your word oh God is a lamp unto my feet and the light to my path. The Lord is my shield, my glory and the lifter up of my head. I commit all my works to the Lord, and He establishes my thoughts. I do not lean on my own understanding; in all my ways I acknowledge Him, and He directs my paths.

My delight is in the Word of God. I am like a tree planted by the rivers of the water that brings forth fruit in its season; whose leaf shall not wither and whatever I do shall prosper. Even in dry seasons, I am fruitful. The Lord supplies me with seed to sow and bread for food. He supplies and multiplies the seed I sow and increases the fruits of my righteousness. I am blessed and highly favored. I shall fulfill destiny in Jesus name Amen!

Theme: Untouchable

Text: Psalm 68:19, Psalm 103: 5,

Isaiah 43:3-4, Psalm 105; 14-15,

Psalm 91 :9-10.

Affirmation

Blessed be the Lord who daily loads me with benefits and satisfies my mouth with good things so that my youth is renewed like the eagle's. I walk in divine health therefore sickness has no place in my body.

Because I have made the Lord who is my refuge even the Most-High my dwelling place, no evil shall befall me neither shall any plague come near my dwelling. I and my family are saved under the shadows of His wings. The mighty hand of God is upon me. His covenant of peace, He shall not alter or break. For He permits no one to do me wrong. Yes, He rebuke kings for my sake saying, "touch not my anointed and do my prophet no harm". He has given Egypt for my ramson and men for me.I am precious in the sight of my Father. I shall fulfill purpose in Jesus name Amen.

Theme: Songs of Deliverance

Text: Psalm 40:1-3, Isaiah 55: 10-12

Affirmation

I waited patiently upon the Lord and He inclined to me and heard my cry. He brought me out of a horrible pit, out of rising and falling and He set my feet upon a rock and established my goings. He has put a new song in my mouth. Praise to our God, many will see this song and will trust in the Lord.

I shall go out with joy and be led out with peace. The mountains and the hills shall break forth into singing before me and all the trees of the field shall clap their hands. Every word the Lord has spoken concerning me shall not return to Him void, but it shall accomplish what the Lord pleases and shall prosper in the thing for which

the Lord sent it. I shall fulfill purpose
in Jesus name Amen.

Theme: My Time! My Season!

Text: Daniel 2:20-22, Daniel 4:3,

Isaiah 60:1, Isaiah 45:3,

Obadiah 1:17

Affirmation

Blessed be the name of God Forever and ever. For wisdom and might are His and He changes the times and the seasons. How great are His signs and how mighty His wonders! He removes kings and raises up kings. It is my season; I arise and shine for my light has come and the glory of God is risen upon me.

He reveals deep and secret things. He knows what is in the darkness; His name is Omniscient. He shall give me treasures in the darkness and secret riches in hidden places. It is my year of possession and greatness, and upon

mount Zion I receive my deliverance
and walk in holiness in Christ Jesus. It
is my time; it is my season! I shall fulfill
purpose in Jesus name Amen.

Theme: Everlasting Blessings
Text: Isaiah 61:7, Isaiah 65:21-23,

Isaiah 43:4.

Affirmation

Instead of my shame I shall have double honor, and instead of confusion I shall rejoice in my portion. Therefore, in my land, I shall possess double; everlasting joy shall be mine. I shall build houses and inhabit them; I shall plant vineyards and eat the fruit. I shall not build, and another inhabit, I shall not plant, and another eat.

For as the days of the tree, so shall be my days and I shall long enjoy the works of my hands. I shall not labor in vain nor bring forth children for trouble for I am the descendant of the blessed of the Lord. It shall come to pass that before I call, the Lord will answer, and while I am still speaking,

He will hear. Since I am precious in His sight, I have been honored and He has loved me. Therefore, He will give men for me and people for my life. I shall fulfill purpose in Jesus name Amen.

Week Thirty-Three

Theme: Empowered to Win

Text: Colossians 3:15-16,

2 Timothy 1:7, 1 John 4:4,

1 Corinthians 15:57,

Galatians 6:9

Affirmation

The Peace of God rules in my heart and the word of Christ dwells in me richly in all wisdom.

For God has not given me the spirit of fear but of love, power and a sound mind. I have the mind of Christ. Greater is He that is in me than He that is in the world. I am more than a conqueror, a world overcomer. Thanks be to God who gives me victory through our Lord Jesus Christ. Therefore, I remain steadfast, unmovable, always abounding in the work of the Lord, for as much as I know that my labor is not in vain in the Lord. I shall not be weary in well doing, for in due season, I shall reap if I faint not. I shall accomplish my vision and mission on earth. I shall not be cut short. I shall fulfill purpose in Jesus name Amen.

Theme: Keeper of My Soul

Text: Psalm 121: 1-8, Psalm 27:5,

Affirmation

I look up to the heavens from where comes my help? My help comes from the Lord who made heaven and earth. He would not suffer my foot to be moved, He that keeps me will not slumber. Behold He that keeps me, and my family shall neither slumber nor sleep. The Lord is my keeper, the Lord is my shade upon my right hand. The sun shall not smite me by day, nor the moon by night. The Lord shall preserve me from all evil: he shall preserve my soul. I am blessed going out, I am blessed coming in.

 As I wait on the Lord, my strength is renewed daily. For in the time of trouble, He shall hide me in His pavilion: in the secret of His tabernacle shall He hide me, He shall set me upon a rock. I am a city set on the mountain top; my light will shine in all the nations of the earth. I shall fulfill purpose in Jesus name. Amen.

Theme: Supernatural Provisions

Text: Revelations 7:16-17,

Isaiah 49:10-11, Isaiah 45: 2-3

Affirmation

Blessing and glory and wisdom; thanksgiving and honor and power and might be to our God forever and ever Amen! I will worship God, all the days and nights of my life. Never again will I hunger, never again will I thirst. The sun shall not strike me, nor any heat. For the Lamb at the center of the throne is my shepherd he will lead me to springs of living water. And God will wipe away every tear from my eyes.

The Lord will make each of my mountains a road and my highways shall be elevated. He shall go before me and make all my crooked path straight. He shall break in pieces the gates of bronze and put in asunder the bars of iron. He will give me the treasures in the darkness and hidden riches of secret places. Provisions are made available to me for my visions. I shall fulfill purpose in Jesus name Amen.

Week Thirty-Six

Theme: Dedicated

Text: 1 Corinthians 6:19,

Romans 12:1-2,

Philippians 4:8,

Philippians 3:13-14

Affirmation

I choose not to defile my body because I am the temple of the Holy Spirit. I present my body as a living sacrifice, holy, acceptable to God which is my reasonable service. I do not conform to the standard of this world but am transformed by the renewing of my mind that I may prove what is good and acceptable and perfect will of God.

I subdue every of my thought in obedience to the word of God. I choose to think of whatsoever things are true, whatsoever things are honest, whatsoever things are just, whatsoever things are pure, whatsoever things are lovely, whatsoever things are of good report. I do not count myself to have apprehended, but one thing I do, forgetting those things which are behind and reaching forward to those things which are ahead. I press forward the goal for the prize of the high calling of God in Christ Jesus. I shall accomplish my mission and achieve my vision. I shall fulfill purpose in Jesus name Amen.

Theme: I am productive
Text: Genesis 1:28,

Deuteronomy 28:3-13

Affirmation

The Lord has commanded me to be fruitful and multiply. Therefore, I am fruitful spiritually, financially, physically, materially and academically.

I obey the Word of God; the blessings of the Lord shall come upon me and overtake me. I am blessed in the city and in the country. I am blessed coming in and going out. The Lord will cause my enemies who rise against me to be defeated before my face. They shall come out against me in one way and flee before me seven ways. The Lord will command the blessing on me in my storehouses and in all to which I set my hands. He will bless me in the land which He has given me. The Lord will establish me as a holy one to Himself. Then all people of the earth shall see that I am called by the name of the Lord and they shall be afraid of me. The Lord will open to me His good treasure, the heavens to give rain to my land in its season and to bless all the work of my hand. I shall lend to nations and not borrow. The Lord shall make me the head and not the tail. I shall be above only and not beneath. I shall fulfill destiny in Jesus name Amen

Theme: Walking in Dominion

Text: Genesis 1:28, 1 Peter 2:9,

2 Timothy 1:7, Romans 8:37,

1 John 4:4, 1 Samuel 30:8,

Ephesians 6:10, Psalm 65:11

Affirmation

The Lord has commanded me to fill the earth, subdue it and take dominion. Therefore, I take dominion in every aspect of my life. I am a royal priesthood, a holy nation, a peculiar person. As I rule in my world, I shall proclaim the praises of God who has called me out of darkness into His marvelous light. I am more than a conqueror; greater is He in me than He that is in the world.

The Lord arms me with strength and makes my way perfect. He makes my feet like the feet of deer and sets me on my high places. He teaches my hands to make war so that my arms can bend a bow of bronze. I pursue and overtake all my enemies and I recover all that has been stolen from me.

I know that all things work together for my good because I love God and because I am called according to His purpose. I am strong in the Lord and in the power of His might. The Lord crowns my year with His goodness; and my paths drip with abundance. I shall fulfill purpose in Jesus name Amen!

Theme: Confident Assurance.

Text: 1 Corinthians 10:13,

Ephesians 3:20-21,

Isaiah 41:10, Isaiah 43:18-19,

Isaiah 62:4

Affirmation

You are my hiding place Oh God, you will protect me from trouble and surround me with songs of deliverance. My God is faithful who will not allow me to be tempted beyond what I am able, but with the temptation will also make a way of escape that I may be able to bear it.

Unto Him who is able to do exceedingly, abundantly above all that I ask or think according to the power that works in me. To Him be glory by Christ Jesus to all generations forever and ever Amen. He shall surely exceed my expectations. I do not fear for God is with me. He will strengthen me, yes, He will help me. He will uphold me with His righteous right hand. I forget the former things; I do not dwell on the past. See God is doing a new thing! He is making a way in my wilderness and rivers in my deserts. I shall no longer be termed forsaken nor my land anymore be termed desolate, but I shall be called Hephzibah and my land Beulah for the Lord delights in me and my land shall be married. I shall fulfill purpose in Jesus name Amen!

Theme: Set Apart for Excellence

Text: Psalm 20:6-9, Psalm 18:1-3,

Psalm 27:4-5, Isaiah 60:15.

Affirmation

I will love you oh Lord; my strength. The Lord is my rock and my fortress and my deliverer. My God, my strength in whom I will trust. My shield and the horn of my salvation, my stronghold. I will call upon the Lord, who is worthy to be praised, so shall I be saved from my enemies. Now I know that the Lord saves His anointed. He will answer me from His Holy heaven, with the saving strength of His right hand.

Some trust in chariots and some in horses, but I will remember the name of the Lord, my God. They have bowed down and fallen, but I have risen, and I stand upright. I know my God; I shall be strong and do exploits. One thing I have desired of the Lord. That I will seek, that I may dwell in the house of the Lord all the days of my life. To behold the beauty of the Lord and to inquire in His temple. For in time of trouble, He shall hide me in His pavilion; in the secret place of His tabernacle. He shall hide me; He shall set me on high upon a rock. The Lord will make me an eternal excellence, a joy of many generations. I shall fulfill purpose in Jesus name Amen!

Theme: My Portion.

Text: Ephesians 1:3, Psalm 16:5-8:11,

Psalm 23 :4; 6

Affirmation

Blessed be the God and Father of our Lord Jesus Christ, who has blessed me with every spiritual blessing in the heavenly places in Christ. Oh Lord, you are the portion of my inheritance and my cup. You maintain my lot. The lines have fallen to me in pleasant places, yes, I have a good heritage.

I will bless the Lord who has given me counsel. My heart also instructs me in the night season. I have set the Lord always before me; Because He is at my right hand, I shall not be moved. He will show me the path of life, in His presence is fullness of joy. At thy right hand are pleasures forever more. Yea though I walk through the valley of the shadows of death. I will fear no evil, for you are with me, Your rod and Your staff they comfort me. Surely goodness and mercy shall follow me, all the days of my life, and I will dwell in the house of the Lord forever. I shall fulfill purpose in Jesus name Amen!

Theme: Rooted in Christ.

Text: Colossians 2:6-7,

Psalm 91: 9-11; 14-16

Affirmation

As I have received Christ Jesus the Lord, so I walk in Him, rooted and built up in Him and established in the faith as I have been taught, abounding in it with thanksgiving; Because I have made the Lord who is my refuge, even the Most high my dwelling place, no evil shall befall me nor shall any plague come near my dwelling. For He has given His angels charge over me, to keep me in all my ways.

I have set my love upon the Lord; therefore, He will deliver me. He will set me on high because I have known His name. I shall call upon Him and He will answer me. He will be with me in trouble. He will deliver me and honor

me; with long life will He satisfy me
and show me His salvation. I shall
fulfill purpose in Jesus name Amen.

Week Forty-Three

Theme: Satisfied

Text: Psalm 36:7-9, Psalm 37:4,

Psalm 23-24. John 14:6,

Psalm 90:14; 16-17

Affirmation

How precious is Your lovingkindness Oh! God. I put my trust under the shadow of your wings. I am abundantly satisfied with the fullness of Your house. I drink from the river of Your pleasures. For with You is the fountain of life and in your light, I see light.

You are the Way, the Truth and Life. I delight myself in the Lord and He shall fulfill the desires of my heart. My steps are ordered by the Lord and He delights in my way. Though I fall, I shall not be utterly cast down for the Lord upholds me with His hand and

He shall take me from glory to glory. Oh, satisfy me early with your mercy that I may rejoice and be glad all my days. Let your work appear to me and Your glory to my children. Let Your beauty be upon me Oh Lord, my God, and establish the work of my hands. I enter my rest in Christ Jesus name. Amen

Theme: Mighty Hands

Text: Psalm, 40:1-3, 2 Samuel 22:2-3

Affirmation

I waited patiently for the Lord, and He inclined unto me and heard my cry. He brought me up also out of a horrible pit, out of the miry clay, and set my feet upon a rock, and established my goings. He has put a new song in my mouth, even praise unto our God: many shall see it and fear and shall trust in the Lord.

The Lord is my rock, and my fortress, and my deliverer, The God of my rock, in Him will I trust: He is my shield and the horn of my salvation, my high tower and my refuge, my savior, thou saves me from violence. I will call on the Lord, who is worthy to be praised: so, shall I be saved from mine enemies. I am blessed and highly favored. For

out of my belly shall flow rivers of
waters.I shall fulfill destiny in Jesus
name Amen.

Theme: Wisdom Is All.

Text: James 1:1-5, Proverbs 3:14-25,

Proverbs 4:7-9, Proverbs 3:3-4,

Proverbs 4:18.

Affirmation

I count it all joy in my various trials, knowing that the testing of my faith produces patience; but then let patience have its perfect work in me, that I may be perfect and complete lacking nothing.

Wisdom is the principal thing; in all my getting I ask for wisdom oh God! Because in her is length of days, riches and honor, pleasantness and peace, sustainability and life to my soul, grace to my neck, safety and protection. I embrace wisdom today, Lord let my head be an ornament of grace and let a crown of glory be delivered to me. I shall be honored as I embrace wisdom. When I walk, my steps shall not be hindered, and when I run, I will not stumble. I walk in mercy and truth, I bind them round my neck and write them on the tablet of my heart, and so I shall find favor and high esteem in the sight of God and man. My path is like the shining sun that shines ever brighter unto the perfect day. I shall fulfill purpose in Jesus name Amen.

Week Forty-Six

Theme: Redeemed to Reign

Text: Psalm 136:1, Psalm 103:1-5,

Psalm 34:10, Psalm 23:1.

2 Peter 1:3, Revelations 1:6.

Affirmation

I will give thanks to the Lord for He is good for His mercy endures forever. Bless the Lord oh my soul and all that is within me bless His Holy name. Bless the Lord all my soul and forget not all His benefits; who forgives all my iniquities, who heals all my diseases, who redeems my life from destruction, who crowns me with lovingkindness and tender mercies, who satisfies my mouth with good things so that my youth is renewed like the eagle's.

Though the young lion lacks and suffer hunger, but I seek the Lord I shall not lack any good thing. The Lord is my shepherd I shall not want. He has given me all things that pertain unto life and godliness; therefore, I am a partaker of His divine nature. He has loved me and washed me from my sins in His own blood and has made me a king and a priest to His God and Father. To Him be glory and dominion forever and ever Amen.

Therefore, I rule in Jesus and I reign in Christ. I shall fulfill purpose in Jesus name Amen.

Week Forty-Seven

Theme: Everlasting Covenant

Text: Psalm 84:11, Psalm 35:27,
Galatians 3:29, Genesis 12:2-3,
Genesis 15:1, Genesis 17:6.

Affirmation

For the Lord God is my sun and shield, He will give me grace and glory. No good thing will He withhold from me. I will continually say, let The Lord be magnified which has pleasure in my prosperity.

I am the seed of Abraham, an heir according to the promise. I connect to the Abrahamic blessings. The Lord will make me a great nation. He will bless me and make my name great. And I shall be a blessing. He will bless those who bless me and curse those who curse me. And in me all the families of the nation shall be blessed.

The Lord is my shield and exceedingly great reward. The Lord will multiply me. He will make me exceedingly fruitful and will make nations of me, and kings shall come from me. I and the children the Lord has given me are for signs and wonders. I shall fulfill purpose in Jesus name Amen.

Week Forty-Eight

Theme: Blessings of Obedience.

Text: Deuteronomy 28:1-12

Affirmation

I am a doer of the word of God; therefore I am blessed in the city, I am blessed in the country. My children are blessed, my career is blessed, my finances and savings are blessed, my businesses are blessed. Everything I possess and will ever have is blessed.

The Lord shall cause my enemies that rise against me to be smitten before my face; they shall come out against me one way and flee before me in seven ways. The Lord shall open unto me His good treasure, the heavens, to give rain on my land in His season, and to bless my home and all the works of my hands. The trees of my field will yield their fruit and the earth shall yield her increase and I shall be safe in the land.

I will lend to nations and not borrow;
my heart shall fear and be enlarged
because the abundance of the sea shall
be converted unto me. This little one
of mine shall become a thousand, and
this small one of mine a strong nation,
The Lord will hasten it in His time. I
shall fulfill purpose in Jesus name
Amen.

THEME: I am Great.

TEXT: Jeremiah 10:6-7, Romans 8: 15-16, Ephesians 1: 6, Ephesians 2:19, Ephesians 1:13.

There is no one like you Oh Lord. You are great, and your name is great in might. Among all the wise men of the nations and all their kingdoms, there is none like you. You are great and your kingdom is forever.

For I have not received the spirit of bondage again to fear, but I have received the Spirit of adoption. You are Abba Father! I am a child of God, an heir of God, a joint heir with Christ. I have been accepted in the beloved; I am therefore no stranger or foreigner but fellow citizens with the saints and household of God. I am sealed with the Holy Spirit of Promise. I belong to the kingdom of light. No darkness shall comprehend me. I am a city set on the mountain top, a light of the world! My light will shine to every corners of the earth. I shall fulfill purpose in Jesus name Amen.

Week fifty

THEME: No bounds

TEXT: Deuteronomy 28:3, Deuteronomy 12:7, Leviticus: 26:4-6a, Job 8:7, Romans 8:19

The Lord has blessed me and made me a blessing. I am blessed in the city, I am blessed in my workplace. Whatever I lay my hands to do shall prosper. I and my household shall eat and rejoice in all I put my hands to do.

The Lord will give me rain in due season; and the land shall yield her increase and the trees of the field shall yield her fruits and my threshing shall reach unto the vintage and the vintage shall reach unto the sowing time and I shall eat of my bread to the full and dwell in my land safely. The Lord will give me peace in the land. I shall lie down and none shall make me afraid. Though my beginning was small, my later end shall greatly increase. For the earnest expectation of the creation is waiting for my manifestation. I shall fulfill purpose in Jesus name Amen.

THEME: Unbeatable Peace

TEXT: Colossians 2:6-7: 10,Acts 17:28, Philippians 4:6-7, Romans 8:28,Philippians 1:6, Ephesians 6:18.

Affirmation

 I have received Christ Jesus the Lord, so I walk in Him daily, rooted and built up in Him and established in the faith as I have been taught, abounding in it with thanksgiving. I am complete in Him who is the head of all principality and power. In Him I live and move and have my being.

I am anxious for nothing, but in everything by prayer and supplication with thanksgiving, I let my request be made known to God, and the peace of God which surpasses all understanding guards my heart and minds through Christ Jesus.

Surely all things work together for my
good because I love God and I am
called according to His purpose. I am
very confident that He who has begun
a good work in me will complete it
until the day of Jesus Christ. The
grace of my Lord Jesus Christ is with
me. I shall fulfill purpose in Jesus
name Amen.

THEME: I live

TEXT: Romans 8:11, Galatians 2:20b, Ephesians 1:3-13, Galatians 6:17, Ephesians 3:20-21.

Affirmation:

The same Spirit of Him who raised Christ from the dead dwells in me. Therefore, He who raised Christ from the dead will also give life to my mortal body through His Spirit who dwells in me. Every cell, organ, tissue and system in my body lives; none shall be counted dead. The life which I now live in the flesh I live by the faith of the son of God, who loved me and gave Himself for me.

Blessed be the God and Father of our Lord Jesus Christ who has blessed me with every spiritual blessing in the heavenly places in Christ. I have been adopted, forgiven, redeemed, obtained

inheritance and sealed with the Holy
Spirit of promise. Therefore, let no
man trouble me, for I bear in my body
the marks of my Lord Jesus Christ.
The power of God moves mightily in
my life. Now unto Him who is able to
do exceedingly, abundantly above all
that i ask or think, be all the glory
forever and ever. Because He lives in
me, I shall fulfill purpose in Jesus
name Amen.

ABOUT THE AUTHOUR

Sylvia Chekwube Obiefule hails from Imo state, Eastern Nigeria. She is a gospel music singer and a songwriter. She holds a bachelor's degree in Industrial Chemistry and a Diploma in Theology obtained at Christ Restoration Bible College Ohio, United States.

Currently, she serves in the music ministry of Faithway Baptist Church, Brice, Ohio and has the passion to impart generations through songs, writing and preaching the gospel of our Lord Jesus Christ.

She is happily married with children.